The
Girl
in the
Hat

કેંજિ

A

Fool's

Tale

ELI STONEMAN

Contact author at:
estoneman60@gmail.com

ISBN-13: 978-1506100821
ISBN-10: 1506100821

Cover and interior design:
The Publishing Pro, LLC,
Colorado Springs, Colorado

Contents

With Gratitude

To Sue, Bill, and Ken
for all your encouragement

1 | **The Theory**

"I've got a theory," I told my friend.

We'd stopped for a pint on the way home from work. One led to two and two led to my theory.

"We start digging our graves in grade school—each year, each lump from life, each disappointment a little deeper. By the time we reach forty, we try it on for size, climb in, stretch out, maybe get comfortable. Some of us get back out, brush ourselves off, and walk around for a while, never getting too far away. But some of us, yeah, some of us get real comfortable, settle in and start to die, not all at once, mind you, but rather than living, start dying."

I had his attention if not his understanding.

"Then suddenly something might startle you. You jump up, look around, and maybe even climb out, and like waking from a coma, shout 'I'm alive!' When the moment passes and you forget what it was or what it felt like, you lie back down and wait to be buried."

He didn't say anything and we sat in silence, drank our beers, looked away, left away, straight away, down away—just away.

After a few awkward moments, he spoke. "Playing golf this weekend?"

"Nope, gotta work."

I hate whiners, have little patience for complainers and less for outright griping. This being said I must confess to being a bit uneasy telling my tale. I've played it out in my mind endlessly and hope to find some peace by putting it to paper.

2 | Black Dogs and Fedoras

My name is Eli. I'm a fifty-something guy and I'm depressed. There, I said it. The D word. Churchill's "black dog." And no, I'm not drawing comparisons between myself and Winston. I just like his term.

I run a small business that has staggered through the years of the great recession. I've been married to a woman with a debilitating illness for a long time, haven't had sex with anyone but myself in six years, and my golf game is tanking. Sad but true.

I do the shopping; we have a housekeeper, and we eat a lot of takeout. Our friends have made themselves scarce, and our grandchildren have crossed the border of in-law land; we rarely see them.

My wife doesn't get out much, and I work a lot. We had an okay life once, the joys outweighing the sorrows. What more is there? But the sorrows have faded the colors of our being to a dreary gray; we don't smile much anymore. I play a little golf, go through the motions, and get by.

And then something happened.

I met a girl. She wore a gray fedora. Kerry was her name; on stage she was known as Charger. Yep! The damn fool fell for a stripper—rube, maroon, sucker. Of all the idiocy! I know, but hear me out.

I'd been to strip clubs periodically over the years, a little eye candy, the company of scantily clad women a most pleasant diversion, rarely indulged. What drew me this particular evening was different. I'd had a long day, had left home sixteen hours earlier for a couple of days of golfing, a bit of beer drinking, and whatever might come. I don't particularly like the gaming tables or the slots and was feeling a bit down and alone in a casino full of people. I took a walk.

When I walked into the club, the first thing I saw was the hat. She was on the smaller of two stages, lovely, leggy, and blonde. I ordered a water and took a seat.

Looking past her, I was miles away.

Now don't start getting too judgmental on me. I'm no Bob Dylan or even Bob Seger, but they both sang of a similar memory and nobody hates them. Well anyway, I'm sitting there staring out into space, yeah, really, and suddenly she's by my side.

"Like your hat," I blurt.

Now I've never been one for lap dances; makes me feel like a slobbering pervert. Hey, I'm lonely but I still have some dignity. Sensing my unease, she offers me a back rub, at the bar if I'd like. No back rooms, no couches, and okay, my back hurts. Thirty years of hard labor does that, so to the bar we go. Great massage. I pull out a wad of cash; she scoops it up. I've been taken.

She leaves, says she'll be back and disappears. Guess I had it coming. I smile a fool's smile. Funny thing is, she comes back, asks me if I meant to give her so much. Eighty dollars, I say. Eighty-five, says she. I smile and ask her to stay a while.

We talk. She tells me her name, her hobbies, about her day job, where she lives, her brother, her dad, even her grandma, for chrissake. The time goes by so easily. When she leaves to take the stage, she tells me she'll be right back and sure enough, she is. One of her coworkers comes by and suggests I resemble Hemingway. Feeling more like George Babbitt, I laugh.

The time goes by and I begin to feel I've pushed the charade far enough. She was no kid, thirty-five she said, born the year I went on my great adventure with a southern rock band. But still, I wasn't drunk and I knew the silliness of attempting to take this further. She kissed my cheek. Did I owe her for her time? I asked, hoping not to offend, but trying in an awkward way to do the right thing.

"No, Hon, we're good." And we walked our separate ways.

My single attempt at therapy came years ago when, dealing with an earlier bout of middle-aged angst, I baited my friend Dr. Bob, a regular guy and child psychologist. "Buy a Porsche," he said. I didn't, couldn't, and yet found my way as I suppose he meant I should.

I walked away that night, at ease. I thought of her as I lay my head down, thought of her more the next day, and so on for the next several weeks, an out-and-out goddamn obsession. I fantasized every aspect of her being, her life in faraway western New York, her life with me, without me, the things I should have said, the things I'd like to have shared with her. I walked through my days dreaming, dreaming the kind of dreams one has about winning the lottery. People began to notice, to question.

So here I sit, trying to purge myself, haunted by a tingle I'd not felt for thirty years, unreal, half imagined, yet based on something real. I'd allowed myself to become the embodiment of Thoreau's men living lives of quiet desperation, a somber, lethargic death march. Just like that, part of me had been jerked awake, given a thirst for life, love, a little bit of happiness. I'll never really know. This girl, wearing my grandfather's hat—I've imagined her six ways to Sunday. I'll never have a cup of coffee with her, a beer, a conversation. I'll never see her again yet I will never forget her, for like a first love, she has changed me, this sweet, sexy, beautiful siren.

All right, I hear you. "The damn fool fell for a stripper."

Yeah, I did.

But tell me, were she a waitress, a clerk, a nurse, a fishmonger, would the chorus still sing nay?

Well that's it, my whining saga of lost love, youth, opportunity. And who cares? The world is full of people with real troubles—famine, war, death, sickness. I'm fifty-one and healthy, can outwork and outdo most guys half my age. I have a nice home, enough to eat, good friends, and a business that with a little tweaking should be all right. I've never been to jail and try my best to do right. In the scheme of things I'm a lucky man.

I've reconnected with a cousin a few years younger than I who had a rather successful career as a dancer. She's beautiful, financially secure, confident, and nice. I'd always liked and admired her and, though we'd become estranged over time, her career choice was never a thing I sought to judge. She is a woman who capitalized on her God-given beauty with grace and charm and today enjoys a lucrative second career, more conservative in nature, and her life is good.

So please don't judge me too harshly, this old fool and his aching heart. Kind of like a kid who didn't get what he wanted for Christmas. I'll get over it. And in the meantime, I'll continue to seek rainbows, and if the gold ring passes my way again, perhaps I'll grab it before it kisses my cheek and walks away. Maybe I'll hold it in my hand and savor its glow for more than just a few lousy minutes.

Yeah, maybe.

3 | The Essay

That was the essay, 1,500 to 1,700 words, written for a section of the *New York Times* called "Modern Love." I admit hoping it would be so overwhelmingly compelling that someone, somewhere, would read it, recognize her, alert her to this pained soul who pined for her. She'd reach out and ...

Okay, I was out of my mind, so much so that I had no focus for weeks— hell, maybe months—after being completely shaken by a peek at life beyond the rock pile. I sought counsel.

Jed was a counselor by trade. He'd worked with my wife and knew what I was dealing with. He'd also worked with my grandson when the kid lived with us. The kid's parents were a mess, he'd missed 150 days of school at the age of twelve, and was remanded to our care in the form of custodial guardianship. He lived with us for two

years. At his insistence I engaged in a cus-
tody battle with his rat of a father that cost
me twenty grand, only to have him change
his mind a year later. I haven't spoken to
him in nine months.

Anyway, back to Jed. He read my essay,
seemed to enjoy it. Jed was a good guy. He
stood about five feet tall, was bearded like
me, about seventy. He was easy to talk to
and kept it simple. If I heard him correctly, he summed it up as a mid-life thing. All
right, no surprise there but shit, I thought
I'd been through all that at forty. I'd been
dealt a bad hand with the wife's men-
tal state. This girl represented my fading
youth.

"You need to find this girl," Jed said.

"Yes!" I agreed emphatically.

"Or maybe you should just get yourself
a piece," he amended.

"Yeah," I said, although with less enthu-
siasm.

This wasn't about sex. Well, maybe a
little. Besides, some years before I'd gone
that route, things got messy, ended badly,

and—forget it, I don't want to go there now.

I saw Jed several times. He encouraged me to pursue publication, perhaps as a release, and concluded that my sense of honor and conscience would prevent me from any course of action that would hurt the wife. Christ—the old Catholic-boy syndrome.

So I worked and reworked the essay, showed it to my buddy—you know, the guy at the bar. He liked it. Showed it to my neighbor Bill.

Bill is a writer. I've talked to him about his avocation several times, and I'm still not sure what the hell he writes about, academics, something or other. I like Bill. He just had his eightieth birthday, frequently rides his bike as I'm walking the dogs, and we talk baseball. Mostly. Hailing from Massachusetts, he's a Red Sox fan, but I don't hold that against him. Hell, it gives us something to talk about.

Well, Bill enjoyed my essay and wrote me this note. The man writes well. I was humbled.

Dear Eli:

Thanks for sharing this piece with me. Heartfelt words filled with hope, what might be, and also acceptance of life as is and although not easy, one you are proud of. Isn't it great that one experience, a few moments of time, can give one such relief, a taste of excitement, wonder, and being worthy of a returned affection? Being liked and feeling that all the way to our bones.

It is, as you say, a struggle to keep alive and out of the grave, which has a compelling allure to it. Death does seem at times to be the only way we can find peace with our daily struggles. It's a battle to go on. As the writer Foote (forget his first name) suggests, "When I look at what people go through, the pain, problems, loss, it's amazing to me how they go on. But in the end that's all we can do, go on."

So this is a great step in talking/ writing about how *you* go on and it will resonate with many people who have the same feelings, dilemmas, and sometimes loss of hope. I know it does for me. Thanks for letting me know you. You'll be OK. You write very well, a gift.

Bill

Mighty damn nice of the man. Did he really think it was any good? I don't know but he showed himself to be a true human being and for that I will always be grateful. He also referred me to Sue, a gal who did some editing for him. I sent it off; she responded positively and encouraged me to submit it, said it was worthy of publication as it stood, and corrected some of my atrocious punctuation but left the story intact.

And so I did.

I fancied myself a writer as a young man, took some basic composition at the community college level, had some great encouragement from a professor named Phil Clement. I fancied him to have been a product of the Beat Generation. He was passionate, animated, unlike any teacher I'd ever encountered. Three-hour sessions in the second-floor classroom two-nights-a-week in midsummer. The man gave all he had, looking as though he might collapse from exhaustion by the closing moments of our class.

He told me I had *talent*, a hell of a thing

to tell a nineteen-year-old who'd smoked, tripped, and Quaaluded his way through high school. "You have the talent to be a writer," to be more precise, written in red letters across some meaningless assignment I'd penned. I half believed it, carried a pad at all times, scribbling nonsense. I got an audition at a local newspaper, got the flu on the eve of my assignment, bombed magnificently, and finally ended my nascent career as a "writer."

When I had my heart broken at the age of twenty-two, depressed, alone, and at as low a point in my life as I've known, I filled a notebook with enough drivel of the whining, suffering, romantic sort that I put down the pen and wrote no more. Whining, suffering, romantic drivel? Haven't gone very far, have I?

Thirty years ago a girl silenced my voice and thirty years later another brought it back.

I submitted my story, typing it out with one finger on my I Phone. It took me three-and-a-half hours. Suffering artist! I couldn't point for a week!

And then I waited. It took me eight weeks to write, edit, seek encouragement, and eventually type this thing I did not quite understand but needed to express. It's said that time heals— or is it thyme that heals? A steaming bowl of the stuff with your head under a blanket? I don't know, but the mania subsided. I didn't forget, I just accepted, a sort of resignation. I lay back in the grave, so to speak, buried myself with the dirt of work, and the time passed. I got rejected and stuffed it in a drawer.

4 | The Golf Trip

A year goes by. A year and a month, as it were. Golf trip to Atlantic City, my friends and I. Let me explain—I like golf a lot but if I had to golf alone or with people I was indifferent to, well, I don't like golf that much. I golf because I like the guys I golf with.

At one time it seemed I'd never have friends like those I had when coming of age, through high school and up until they started dispersing across the continent and settling into married bliss. I married at twenty-nine, though we'd been together since I was twenty-four, and spent my twenties hanging with, for the most part, beer buddies and such. I saw my old friends, those who'd stuck around, but our hanging out days had ended. I'd still see one or two on a regular basis, get in a bit of trouble over a pint or a few, maybe a ball game, but until I began golfing I was lacking that sense of camaraderie I'd known as a boy. We never really grow up.

My buddies and I are all contractors. We work a lot, sneak out to the golf course when we can, as much as we can, and look forward to three days in A. C. every spring. We stay at a casino, eat at Angelo's, golf 'til we drop, and then hit the casino. "We waited all year; we'll sleep when we go home."

Problem is, I hate the casino. I wander around until I invariably find myself seeking some fresh air, not about to succumb to the charms of Sports Channel in my hotel room. I wander down the boardwalk and end up you know where.

You see, she lived upstate. She came down only sporadically to work here. It's been a goddamned year. "You can't go home again." Faulkner? Wolfe? I always confused the two. But no, I just had nowhere else to go and thought I'd kill an hour or two. And so I did.

It was a busier night in late May than I had seen the April before. Girls came and went. I brushed them off, not interested in padding their ... well, not interested in more than casual observation. I like to look, yeah, but I was sober and I found no real attraction, not enough, anyway. I passed the time watching the human comedy, drunken youngsters fawning, drooling, spilling beer, a couple old guys like me—God, do I look that pathetic? And the ladies.

Two hours went by or so it seemed. I was bored, tired, and thinking of ... Sweet Jesus, it was her! Out of the corner of my eye, it was the hat! I squinted. Some twenty-five feet away on a side stage. Nah, must be some other chick with a hat. Shook me up though. And then, crossing the room, taking center stage ... Goddamn, it was her!

I watched her in rapt amazement, spinning on the pole with athleticism, style, and grace. The hat was white, not the gray I remembered from the first time. The stunned look I wore caught her attention. She finished her dance, collected her dollar-bill tributes, and, never taking her eyes off me, made her way to where I sat, plopped herself into my lap, and smiled.

"It's you," I stammered. You'd think with all the wordy nonsense I've weaved onto the preceding pages, I might have said something more elegant, thoughtful, cool, for fuck's sake. But no, "It's you" was all I could do. I tried to explain, to convey the depth of my story, the how, the why, the fucking meaning of life.

But it was loud, it was noisy, and she had to work.

She remembered, or so she said, parts of the story of our first meeting, didn't seem surprised that I knew bits and shards of her life. I was holding in my lap the object of my previous year's absolute obsession and damn it, I couldn't let go.

She had to go back to work; she left me. I watched her work the room, watched her dance, saw her disappear with— well, let's be real, I fell for a stripper. Last time I was very nearly the only guy in the place. To-night there was money to be made.

I waited and, as I did, I realized there would be no time for quiet conversation of the type I'd known before. You know, despite the atmosphere, the dancing, the everything else, it was the beauty of the girl, not the girl's beauty, that I had been taken with.

The only way I would get a few moments with her, moments I had never thought I'd see again, would be to succumb to the back room and the dreaded lap dance. I figured I could just play it down, ask her to sit with me. The price was thirty dollars for five minutes, one hundred dollars for twenty minutes. "Twenty minutes," I nearly shouted.

She squeezed my hand and led me away. I told her who I was, how I'd enjoyed her company. She told me she liked me, didn't get too many "nice guys." I ate it up, and when she began to ride me like a champ, I was overwhelmed.

She treated me with the heaviest dose of passionate, fiery intimacy I'd ever known. I told her I'd do massive amounts of Viagra to be her lover.

She said, "Baby, you don't need any Viagra."

And as a smile passed across our hero's

face, he was ecstatic to be able to agree.
When he bit her boob and recoiled in hor-
ror, apologizing—"You can't be walking
around with bite marks!"

"It's okay, Baby, that was just a nibble."

I asked to see her face in ecstasy and to
my dying day I will think I did as she rode
my thigh.

I told her I would not climax. She seemed
disappointed, perhaps a little impressed.
"You have that control?" she asked before
moaning softly in my ear.

We would be wonderful lovers, I told her,
and meant it with all that I was or would
ever be. You know, this happened with one
of us fully clothed, and despite her heroic
efforts I kept my word—not now, not like
this.

I made my best pitch. "Could this ever
happen for real?"

"Sometimes," she cooed into my ear with
heavy breath, "but I have to get home to my
daughter."

"Good reason," said I. "We would be
wonderful lovers ..."

I said good night and left, starstruck at the strangeness and wonder of it all. Well, maybe it's not so strange, but I never expected it, that second chance I'd dreamed of, the type of shit that just doesn't happen—it happened. I got to say much of what I wanted to say the year before and because I cared for her, there was some validity to the fantasy. If there had been no genuine feeling in the intensity of her lovemaking, then the real thing would probably kill me—and a hell of death it would be.

The madness begins anew.

I thought hard all the way back. When I returned, I thought and searched for a way to move on—and chose to write her a letter, fan mail if you would, a continuation of the conversation. Did I think she would remember me? Probably not, but with a nudge, maybe. If I could write a letter of humor, simple human yearning ... who knows?

So here's the letter. You've heard most of the story already but you tell me—I had a human connection, tenuous but real. I thought I'd grow old never knowing another moment. I got my second chance. What, if anything, could yet come? Nothing, perhaps, but we shall see.

5 | The Letter:

Kerry,

Guy walks into a bar, quiet Sunday night, late April, long day, heavy of heart. Guy meets girl, girl with a hat, lovely and sweet. She offers a dance, he accepts a back rub. Done, she scoops up his cash, kisses his cheek, and walks off. Twice the price offered; he smiles, not really minding. "Guess I had it coming," he thinks. Lost in his thoughts, he senses her presence. "Did you mean to give me that much?" she asks. "Eighty bucks," says he. "Eighty-five," says she. They both smile.

She sits beside him and they begin to talk. He hails from eastern Long Island, she from western New York State. She tells him of her day job, her grandma, a trip to Florida with her brother (yeah, the sunburn story). They talk for hours. Born the year he traveled to Florida with a rock band, she was no kid but still young enough.

Afraid he'd been making a fool of himself, he gets up, says goodnight. She kisses his cheek again and he walks off into the night.

On a golf trip with some buddies, he walks into a casino full of people, never feeling more alone. Been married to a woman crippled by depression for a long time, he nurtured her emotionally and financially, trying to be a good man and live with the emptiness of being alone.

He returned from his trip with thoughts of the girl in the fedora. Waking up, he thought of her. Trying to work, he thought of her. Most waking moments, she was present. She had stirred in him something long dead or at best dormant. He regretted its passing, buried himself in work, and got on with his life.

A year goes by. Guy walks into a bar, meets girl in hat, and it starts again. I ask you, is there anything more normal? Guy meets girl, girl is beautiful, girl is fun, sassy, and someone you would open your heart to. If it happened in another venue …. Well, it didn't, it happened there, and I'm a goddamned customer.

Well, now I'm home, back to running my business, or trying to. You see, just like last year I wake up to her face, her smile, her damned hat. The rest of her was mighty nice as well, but her persona was for real. Dr. Phil in heels and a bikini. You know who the sirens were? "They tempted brave Ulysses whose naked ears were tortured." So said Cream. They tempted mariners with

their beautiful songs 'til they crashed
their ships upon the rocks.

Please excuse me. I started this
letter earlier today at a job site and am
completing it in my office with a bottle of
Chianti.

I ain't no white knight. She don't need
saving, not as far as I can see. She's
strong. Christ, I wish the bums working for
me had half her stamina. She's smart and
like my sister, who danced for over twenty
years, she's nobody's fool. I ain't no cash
cow; I live 300 miles away. I just found
her to be the embodiment of something I
knew once and seemed to have forgotten with
the passage of time.

I'm a bit delirious. I played 108 holes
of golf in four days, was up until 3:30 on
Monday night, and got up every day at 6:00
A.M. Came home with a respiratory infection,
nineteen messages from customers on my
phone, and had to fire a guy this morning.
Yet all I can think of is her— the fantasy
blurring the lines of reality?

So what do I do? Last year I eventually
got over it, never forgetting but settling
back into my sleepwalk of a life. This
year—shoot—I make a damned fool of myself
and write her a letter. Why? Because if I
didn't, I'd always wonder what would have
happened if I did. All the things I wish
I'd said, I'm trying to say. Maybe I'll

get back to my zombie-like state, go to work six days, sixty-five to seventy hours a week, and bury her memory. I expect so. But maybe she'll write me back, just to call me a damned old fool or worse. But hell, I had to get it out and here it is.

I don't know if this is acceptable or considered creepy, scary, or worse. I hope it doesn't make her uncomfortable. I hope if she has a laugh with her friends over this, she is kind to me. And Christ, I hope most of all that she responds to me, a letter, an email. And if she doesn't, who knows, I may walk into that bar next year after a lonely walk on the boardwalk and see the hat, the girl, the … Yeah.

By the way, I mentioned a film to you, *The Unbearable Lightness of Being*, **1988**, Daniel Day Lewis, Lena Olin, Juliette Binochet. Lena Olin in a bowler. You might be amused.

Eli-- White Beard

P.S.: I like to write and would welcome your friendship and maybe a shared smile.

Mailed on Tuesday at 6:30 P.M. It is now Friday, 8:30 P.M. I expect she's read it. Would she respond?

What if it never got there? What if some

leering idiot in the post office noticed the addressee, the club she worked, and opened it, sharing a hearty laugh with his simian friends? What if it got lost, the club manager threw it into the pile of other pathetic …? All right, this is damned silly. This was my one shot, one letter, one pitch. What the hell would I say if she did respond? What indeed?

6 | The Year She Was Born

I thought back to the year she was born. I had long hair, drove a VW beetle, got dumped by Allison, old blue eyes. "You're burnt," she said. Damned if I wasn't. I'd probably tripped some thirty-odd times the summer before, smoked a lot of weed, and Quaaludes? Strange coincidence but my birthday is 7/14.

I hung out with a bunch of musicians, traveled the local bar scene as they played on weekends. When they left for Florida, rented a house, and invited me to join them, I quit the job I didn't like much, packed my Volkswagen to the roof, dragged another guy with me, and on a Saturday morning in January of 1979 we were off—with an ounce of sensimilla, a bag of black beauties and, within half an hour of being on the road, a case of Molson Golden.

Twenty-eight hours in a VW, seats

pushed forward to accommodate our possessions. It was a two-speed automatic, no clutch; push down on the shifter, and it would engage and you'd shift at about 35 mph. The genius I drove with couldn't grasp this and woke me to shift for him when, while he was driving, the need arose.

We stopped in Florence, South Carolina, at a Howard Johnson's the next morning and when we came out, the car would not start. And, son of a bitch, the battery is under the back seat. We unloaded the car, our possessions piled in the parking lot, solicited a jump, and luckily it started. My friend, Steve was his name, got to talking to some guys from Georgia and spent damn near all his money on an ounce of the worst hashish I had ever smoked. You wouldn't have gotten high if you'd eaten it all at once, smothered in heroin. It was green, for God's sake!

We drove on, never again shutting off the engine, for at least twelve hours. We arrived at our destination about 8:30 Super Bowl Sunday. Shorter season, game was played earlier. It's been thirty-five years; this is how I remember it.

When we'd settled on leaving New York for Florida, there were five guys living there. When we arrived we became numbers nine and ten. We walked in and Steve immediately got bit on the ass by the resident Doberman pinscher, Pamby. I made a pile of my winter coats and such on the floor, covered it with a blanket, and, exhausted, went to sleep.

My roommate was Kevin. Kevin, my lifelong friend. I miss him, haven't seen him in a year. He'd had triple bypass, nearly died. I spent three hours in his hospital room. The bond was still there. We'd been close; I still think we are but, never one to return or make calls, he's gone another way of late.

But back in '79 he was the guy who convinced me I had to go to Florida. He was a persuasive guy and what the hell, I was going nowhere anyway. Kevin had come into my life a few years earlier. I was a child, didn't smoke, listened to top forty music, W-A-A-A-BC. He was not. Kevin smoked

Winstons, had four older brothers and an older sister, had come up hard, introduced me to the Allmans, Derek and the Dominoes (I've worn out three LPs and a CD), weed and my mom's medicine cabinet. He was angry, a bit of a bully, although I was his match physically. He was Fred to my Barney.

We bonded over women (he got them, I didn't) and drugs. The first time I dropped acid he was among the group and we meshed. We knew each other's minds inside out and have been brothers ever since. He's become an outspoken advocate of right-wing politics and considers me a *liberal*. He's hard to converse with now as most conversations turn eventually to the right and wrong of our thinking. Maybe that's why I don't hear from him. As I said, I miss him.

I awoke the next day in a four-bedroom, one-bath house with mattresses and makeshift beds spread throughout. Hindu Ed, a nickname inspired by his style of guitar play, had his own room. Andy the bass player; Brian the drummer; their two buddies (all from Travers City, Michigan, the Cherry Capital of the World) shared a room; a guy named Steve, whom I knew vaguely (I don't know what his connection to the band was or how he got there); and my driving companion, Steve, shared another room. And Dana Piper, the downstairs bedroom. Piper, the lead guitarist, played a 57 Les Paul Junior; he did all the hardest leads, was fifty pounds overweight, lazy, shiftless, and a thorough con man. Ten years older than the rest of us, he was a likeable, irresponsible bum who never held a job for more than a week. He lived to play guitar, get high, and play guitar some more. Man, could he play!

The house was located in the red-light district of St. Petersburg, across the alley from Fred's Good Time Bar and some other joint with a name that eludes me today. There were hookers, gunshots late in the evening, and on the weekends the black clientele spilled out into the street. We made odd neighbors.

Our house was the scene of nightly band practice, nine or ten o'clock until whenever. The living room was filled with drums, the P.A. system, guitar stands, and most evenings, an assortment of musicians, chicks, and hangers on. It was a non-stop party, though some of us had to work; we were not all blessed with the gift of music.

Kevin set Steve and me up with jobs. The city of St. Petersburg was building a sewage treatment facility. It was on a ten-acre-plus site, sandy and barren, not a tree or bit of shade to be had. We were handed shovels and put to work. The contractors who were running the job were from Birmingham, Alabama. Some guy named Cecil, with a red face and a blond perm, was in charge, but our immediate superior was the foreman. His name was Jerry. Jerry was a retired Army Corps of Engineers master sergeant. He had great posture and never called me anything but "Yank." He was a decent sort, though, and I liked him. We were the only white laborers. Our black coworkers eyed us with a mixture of contempt and suspicion; so did the rednecks, for that matter. It sucked working there.

After two weeks I went out for lunch, drove to a condo project on the beach, got hired on the spot for a buck an hour more than I'd been making, and never went back. I now worked on a five-story high-rise, carrying and distributing sheetrock and steel studs, watching the girls and the dolphins all day.

This was the first time away from home for most of us. Some of us worked, some starved, some of us worked and starved. Hindu Ed came home one day to find his door broken off the hinges and his peanut butter and a loaf of bread gone. Hindu Ed also got pinched at Wynn Dixie for stealing a package of Oscar Meyer ham. The fact that he had forty bucks on him didn't help his cause.

Kevin threw Brian the drummer through the back door just off the kitchen when Brian made a move on Kevin's scrambled eggs. Those of us with jobs got paid on Friday, cashing our checks at the local liquor store.

We purchased a bottle of bourbon and made a beeline for Duff's Smorgasbord, all you could eat for $5.95. Waking up most Mondays with the proverbial pocket full of change, sometimes we didn't eat for days.

Steve and I had a thing. I was never much of a thief but my moral compass had no issue with eating stolen food. I would buy vegetables, and Steve would steal the meats. He was amazing; I saw this guy walk out with multiple London broils stuffed in his shirt on half a dozen occasions. He never got nabbed.

It was one thing to procure the food, another to actually cook and eat it. When you live in a house full of ravenous guys who haven't eaten in days, it's no small thing to cook and consume a meal without the potential for violent confrontation.

I lived this way for two months—drank, smoked, roadied on the band's gigs, shot a lot of pool, met a girl from Michigan. Kevin quit his job, joined the unemployed rabble, "them" to the working "us."

I got sick, spent two days with a high

fever, my throat so red it ran blood; no shit, I could have died, and I think I'd have gone unnoticed by my housemates. I'd had enough by then, and on the third day I rose, collected my previous week's paycheck, and told Steve I was out of there. He wanted in. We bade whoever was present a hasty good-bye. We passed Kevin, who'd rear-ended some old guy downtown, on our way to the bridge to Tampa, and we were on our way.

I was still pretty damned sick, which left a greater part of the driving to Steve. I fell asleep on I-95 south of Richmond and woke up to our being nearly out of gas in West Virginia. We spent the night beside the single pump of a general store on some mountain about ten miles off the highway. We had been traveling in a westerly direction. It had taken twenty-eight hours to reach Florida. It took us forty-three hours to return.

We crossed the George Washington Bridge sick, broke, and beaten on St. Patrick's Day. I cursed myself for my foolishness. How could I have been so stupid? Years later, I hold sacred the great adventure of my youth.

7 | After the Letter

Friday morning, the week after I wrote the letter, nine days since I mailed it. Maybe a week since it would have arrived. My hope fades. I'm beginning to lose the spring in my step. I made a play, reached for the ring, and maybe like the machine that checks my lottery tickets says, "Sorry, you are not a winner."

I'd shown the letter to two of my closest friends, the guy at the bar, Evan, and Fitz, another golf buddy whom I liked and found easy to converse with. I'd ambushed Evan that Tuesday evening, half expecting his encouragement and yet fearing a cock of the eyebrow, a twist of the head, a long pause, a suggestion that I'd passed the tipping point of reason.

He looked at me and said, "You gotta send this." He gently reminded me that he was fully aware of my situation at home,

my dedication, my devotion, and my un-
happiness. He was my roommate on the
last seven golf trips and had been following
the story since day one.

I rented a PO Box and checked it daily.
An email would have hit me sooner.

I was not as close with Fitz, but I liked
him. He was the most educated, liberal, and
quirky guy among our group. He struggled
mightily with the game but came back week
after week for more. The general consensus
was that Fitz was a good egg. A photogra-
pher by training, he'd lived fast, partied
hard. He left the excitement of trendy NYC
for the quiet sanctuary of the North Bend.

I asked Fitz to do a photo of me. Fully
expecting Kerry to write, to want clarifica-
tion of just who I was, I needed to be ready.
Every photo of me in the last fifteen years
was one of me in a large chair with a newspaper in my lap or, a few back, a baby or
a toddler. Invariably I was in my chair. I
asked Fitz to make me appear vibrant, vir-
ile, vigorous. He snapped away, said he'd
work on it.

Fitz knew nothing of my story. I showed him the letter. He read it; he reflected on it. "I respect you for taking action," he said.

He spoke of lost opportunities, loves. He'd never been married, lived alone; he understood. He showed me a glimpse of a work of his. I liked it. I've grown closer with Fitz. I hope his golf game improves.

Fitz showed me one of the shots he'd taken of me. "You look a bit like Hemingway." I laughed, shared the passage in my story, and we both laughed. I was not trying to look like Papa, Hemingway or otherwise.

Fitz also touched on the subject of Karl Jung, got a bit heavy and said my actions had caused things to happen, not fate or luck, something to that effect. "You had to do this," he said, "and should be proud."

I'd gone to both these guys feeling the part of delusional nut and came away with encouragement and support. Thinking they'd hold me to the shackles of convention, they'd set me free.

Well, thanks for listening. It's been twelve days and no response, and I'm beginning to accept that it ain't happening. I go to the post office or look for an email much like I look at that damned lottery vending machine. For a fleeting moment my dreams flicker and then, "Sorry, not a winner."

I had more of a chance here, though. I made my pitch and rereading it, I wouldn't have changed much. It reminded me of my days as a fisherman; before golf, my passion was the rod and reel. Alone with my thoughts, I enjoyed many a sunup and down, but most of all the tranquil starry nights standing chest deep in dark waters.

There were times when I stood among a school of stripers so thick they bumped my knees. They'd hit nothing I threw at them and then the tide would change and bang, couldn't miss. Maybe I'd missed the tide with the girl. Maybe had my letter arrived at a different time in her life, I'd have hit my mark.

Maybe life is just that way. What the hell would I have done if she had gotten back to me? Made her my pen pal? Maybe she would have twisted me around her finger, toying with me, teasing. I still don't know what I really wanted from her. Well, yeah, that. But emotionally— shoot, when she landed in my lap I was speechless.

Remember the Old Man and the Sea? Poor sap gets the catch of a lifetime, only to have it reduced to bare bones before he could return to port. Or my favorite loser of all time, Yuri Zhivago. Heroic? Tragic? Romantic? The guy lives through the World War, two revolutions, a civil war, wanders about the frozen Russian steppes, and after thirty years he's riding a bus and looks out the window to see the love of his life walking on the street. He gasps, staggers to the door, and croaks on the sidewalk within twenty-five feet of her. She never notices. Poor bastard knows beauty, writes beautiful poetry, gets a taste of happiness and wham, two-by-four upside the head. Starry-eyed dreamer guys like us just don't get the ring.

So I'm done. If anything happens I'll let you know. Evan says maybe I should go back, put in an appearance. I fear I'd be viewed as a stalker—but maybe.

In the meantime I'll try to keep the dream alive, buy a couple lottery tickets a week, play a little golf, and work a lot. If I've learned anything from this, it's that writing about it has kept it alive and that life, though sometimes cruel, can and does surprise; maybe last of all, that much as the girl was the focus, the story was me, the changes I need to make, and how I have to keep reaching. And maybe I'd rather be poor Doctor Zhivago and have known and felt beautiful things than a guy who had it all and never knew it.

8 | Coming Undone

OK, so I'm not done. I can't let go, not yet. I've been asking myself what I would say if she did respond. What might she say?

"Hi, this is Kerry. Who are you?"

"Hi, this is Kerry. I liked your letter. Tell me about yourself."

"Hi, this is Kerry. No one's ever written a letter like that to me before."

"Hi, this is on behalf of Kerry. If you bother our employee/client again, we will take action."

"Hey, asshole, don't you know when the show is over?"

Been fourteen days since I mailed my letter, twenty-two days since our last encounter. The prospect of her responding fades by the day. I have, though, figured out what it is I want from her. If she were to appear on my email amidst the blueprints and bullshit—or a little ding on my phone, "Who are you and what do you want?"—I know what I will say: "What color are your eyes?"

What color are your eyes? So much to know, so much to ask. I know she's a true blonde, yeah, I know, but her eyes could be blue, maybe hazel. My money's on green. I've never seen her in the light and didn't ask. Seems a good place to start. Would I think of her "windows" as the color of spring—renewal, freshness, no more goddamn snow? Would they be the color of robins' eggs, September skies? Remember 9-11? Not a cloud in sight, one hundred miles away I looked to the sky in amazement at what such beauty had evil traversed. Brown would be autumn. Would she have brown or hazel eyes? Would I ever know?

And then what? I'd want to … . That's just it—I don't know. I've imagined a meeting—I won't call it a date—a meeting halfway, Manhattan, perhaps. I'd take her to lunch, maybe a walk in the park, maybe

a ride on the carousel. Maybe we'd just—
yeah, maybe we'd .... .

I just have no plan.

9 | The Best Laid Plans

I had plans once. I got the opportunity to become a plumber at the age of 26, an old "helper," as most other neophytes of the trade were in their late teens. I had been building swimming pools, hard work with a dim future, a young man's job. Guys in their forties pushing wheelbarrows and playing the banjo – a euphemism for shovel work – were not a pretty picture.

Within my first week of plumbing, I learned to do faucets and secured my first moonlighting job. I saw opportunity. I worked nights, weekends, and by the time I was thirty was able to buy a house. By the age of thirty-one, I had a master plumber's license. By thirty-two I was on my own, an entrepreneur. It might also be noted that I had left my druggie days behind. Acid, mescaline, and mushrooms had given way to a serious cocaine habit. A near brush with serious prison time had cured me of my desire to be around dealers and their wares. I've done no more than smoke a little weed in twenty-seven years.

At thirty I said to myself— and I remember this— "All I want out of life is a little house, a small business, and a small boat. By forty I had it all. I had also wanted another TR-6. I had one from my mid- to late-twenties, but that was gravy. To this day I ache when I see one and know the sound of its muffler as it shifts. I close my eyes and remember the thrill.

I miss the thrill—any thrill. Maybe that's why I scribble long into the night about someone I barely know, have only a skeletal connection to. Christ, I've seen every inch of this woman's body and can't tell you the color of her eyes. Pour me another glass of chianti.

Got a lot to be thankful for—nice house, detached office, decent business, good friends, and my health. I'm in pretty decent shape. I've lost about ten pounds since Atlantic City—those dam full-length mirrors in hotel rooms have prompted me to cut out the cookies, desserts, and second or, for that matter, third helpings of my recent past. I work hard, can put any of my employees to shame, can drop down and do fifty pushups with little effort. I walk eighteen holes once or twice a week and often carry my bag.

10 | The Family Way

I am blessed. At the age of fifty-two my dad was on an oxygen machine, could no longer go up a flight of stairs, and had begun his losing battle with emphysema. He was twenty-nine when I was born, had then what was called chronic bronchitis. He was told to quit smoking then or he'd never see me grow up. He did make my wedding, barely; he missed the reception.

A few years back, on one of those starry nights with rod in hand and water gently lapping on the beach, I remembered him. Shit, in some convoluted way I saw his life in bits and pieces, gathered from him, his sister, my mom. His mom died when he was nine. He wore the scars of a spilled pot of coffee across his head, neck, and back. His dad, an immigrant from Binetto, Italy, who rode with Black Jack Pershing across the Texas border country chasing Pancho

Villa, was hit by a bus and killed when my dad was thirteen.

Dad was the youngest of four. His brother enlisted in the army and ended up in China during WW II. My dad ended up bouncing around with various relatives, then sleeping on pool tables in gin mills. He enlisted in the Navy at seventeen and ended up in the brig when he slugged an officer. He stood 5 feet 6 inches and weighed about 130, a Bantam rooster with a temper and quick hands. That got him a dishonorable discharge, which haunted him his entire life. He went back home, Brooklyn, and lived with his sister.

He waited tables at a place in East New York, spent his days at Aqueduct or Belmont, depending on the season, until at age twenty-nine he met my mom. He was a decent sort, liked music. I can see him in my room, black light posters, beer bottle collection, lying on my bed with head phones listening to Zappa. For some reason this freaked out my sixteen-year-old mind, but thinking back, it was a cool moment.

He drove trucks for a living, bread truck
size, sometimes for health food compa-
nies, candy, bootleg records, and when I
was young, diapers. He sometimes waited
tables at night and on weekends. He never
made much money, always loved the ponies, and would drink himself silly on a six-
pack of cheap beer most nights. He enjoyed
the good stuff but had a Schmidt's budget.
He taught me an appreciation for film—and
music from Benny Goodman to Hank Wil-
liams. He loved Joe Namath, the Mets, and
the ponies.

Sometimes, when I was a kid, my mom
would send us somewhere and we'd end up
at Aqueduct. I placed my first bet at about
the age of six. Space Control was the horse.
Damned if it didn't win. You don't forget a
moment like that.

They fought a lot; sometimes, though
usually a happy, sleepy drunk, he'd get
mean. He only slapped me around a couple
of times, but at sixteen I raised a bat to him
and it never happened again.

In his forties we moved from his familiar Brooklyn streets. He struggled, spent a good part of his time at the local O.T.B. I can remember finding him there as I cut classes in high school, both of us where we shouldn't have been but me somehow having the upper hand.

"Here," as he handed me a couple of bucks, "don't tell your mother."

They split up when I was seventeen and into my psychedelic journey. He got an apartment, took me to see *Star Wars*, and moved to San Diego, a place dear to him from his Navy days. He would write me over the next few years, sometimes with a few in him. He had a propensity for self-pity; while he did have a shitty life, sometimes his letters sucked. He had an apartment, a friend named Teddy, and I think he had a girlfriend.

Then he got sick. Forty years of hacking his brains out had become emphysema. He came home to live with his sister. We kind of rekindled a relationship. I loved him but did not quite respect him. I saw him as weak. I was in my twenties and just didn't know what life did to people.

I spent his last week of life at his bedside, getting a phone call at 3:30 A.M. from a nurse on duty that I ought to get there. I listened to a lot of classical music at that time of my life. The hospital was about an hour away. On the way Wagner's *Funeral Music*, an excerpt from the Ring Cycle came on the radio, ominous and fucking weird. I held my dad's hand as he died.

The dawn arose and from something like the twentieth floor of Stony Brook Hospital, I looked across Setauket, Stony Brook, Port Jefferson Harbor, and the Long Island sound and bade his spirit farewell. I was thirty.

Son of a bitch, it hadn't occurred to me until just this moment, but it was the twenty-third anniversary of his passing yesterday.

11 | Ramblin' Man

I don't really mean to ramble—or hell, maybe I do. You see, if I keep this up, I keep the dream alive. I stay above ground, looking about, taking it all in. I fear the moment I stop, I'll fall back in the hole and wake up another year older, on another trip with nothing much to say for myself. What did I do for the past year? Well, let's see, I worked, I worked some more. I met a girl once. She wore a hat.

If I keep writing, then the story has life. Anything can yet happen. I could lie to you, making it up as I go. I could pull a Yuri and die tomorrow and sure as shit, her letter would arrive the next day; you could bank on it.

I wonder if she likes chestnuts. If we walked in the park in winter, I'd want chestnuts. Maybe we'd walk to Rockefeller Center to see the tree. I stood in front of that tree once, about 1983. Standing next to me was Danny Kaye, Hans Christian Andersen himself—frigging Walter Mitty. I looked up—he was pretty tall—and smiled. I nodded. He nodded and smiled back at me. That's my Christmas tree in New York story. I liked Danny Kaye.

⊰⊱⊰⊱

The North Bend is populated by a fair share of well-off people, mostly second-home owners with primary residences in places like Garden City, Manhasset, Manhattan, and my favorite title of pretentious hogwash, Basking Ridge, New Jersey. Just saying it produces a gag reflex in me. I've never been there, and it might be an armpit of a place, but the few stuffed-shirt jerks I've met who rolled it off their tongues with their need to impress—well, if they live there, I don't like it.

Anyway, I'm in a lot of these homes. Their lives seem neat and managed. Their clothes are crisp and stylish. Their kids go to college and have good careers. They vacation frequently, drive nice cars, and they spend their time at the "club." I hate the "club." I've been invited a few times—round of golf, drinks afterwards—never again! People who pat you on the back, shake your hand, and seem genuinely glad to see you when you show up to fix their faucet have a difficult time concealing their discomfort when they encounter their plumber at the "club."

They throw it around a lot. "We'll have to have you to the club," they say, but they aren't my kind of people anyway. If I'm ever found to be wearing a pair of salmon shorts, pink shirt to match with the magic emblem, I would hope and deserve to be struck by a large caliber bullet.

Where the hell did all that come from? I'm an angry guy, I guess. I suffer from a bit of road rage and occasionally let loose on a—and I'll say this—*deserving* customer or employee. My anger or rage has a personal nemesis in the person of former heavyweight contender Gerry Cooney.

Once, years ago, when Cooney was training for a title bout with Larry Holmes, I got on a train in Mineola, going to Sloane Kettering to visit a buddy. Gerry lived in Huntington and trained in Manhattan. I get on the train, look for a seat, and there's this guy stretched out across three of them, a couple of guys sitting in the opposite seats. They all look at me; I look back, shrug my shoulders, and shake my head. At this moment a kid comes up and asks for an autograph. I hadn't realized how big this guy was until he stood up. Was I about to say something stupid? I can't really say, but I might have.

Ten years later I've got a service call set up on a Friday morning, 8:30 appointment. I'm running late. The customers are regular, cool people. Coincidentally, people who had me to the "club." But anyway, I'm about twenty minutes late. I knock on the door. I'm late. I'm stressed, and a bit cranky. A guy I've never seen before comes to the door carrying a baby.

He looks at me and, with some attitude, says, "You're late. We've been waiting for you."

I see red, about to lose it, my jaw clenching, bitter redress rising in my chest.

He breaks into a smile, extends his hand, and says, "Hi, I'm Gerry Cooney."

He had gray hair and was dressed in golfing attire, white if I remember correctly, and was less physically intimidating than I remembered him to be. Anyway, two close encounters. To this day, if I know he's at an event or a guest speaker, I shudder.

∽✌✎

As far as the club goes, maybe the chip's on my shoulder. My good friend Dr. Joe told me his father gave him two bits of advice: Never to buy a two-door car and it is okay not to like people, just do it one at a time. There are good and bad eggs everywhere.

Maybe I'm not that angry a guy. I don't go around punching people and my road rage is mainly contained to yelling at the dummies who cut you off when there's no one behind you for a mile, lost tourists who don't get the fuck out of the road to figure shit out, and worst of all, the tailgater. You tailgate me, I'm gonna fuck with you. Bam!

I hit the brakes, speed up to get away, and if I find you on my ass again, we repeat the process. What the fuck, maybe I *am* angry. My luck it will be good old Gerry on his way to a testimonial. I'm told things happen in threes.

Sixteen days. Maybe I am a bit angry. I worked the last few days with a pick and shovel, laying pipe in the ground, wrestled with a seventy-five gallon beast of a water heater up the stairs, down with the new, until 7:30 last night and hung out in the office until midnight scribbling this nonsense. Maybe I'm just tired.

And as long as I'm getting some things off my chest, I'm going to address three things that really piss me off: men wearing sandals, metric wrenches, and soccer. The latter two should be used in the same sentence as they are both European in nature and have supplanted American tools and the great sport of baseball.

I could give a rat's ass about football and all its rah-rah-rah hype. I have a passing interest in basketball but baseball, America's pastime, is my passion. Every time I see a field of kids playing soccer, running back and forth kicking a goddamned ball, I cringe and want to kick their parents' asses.

Metric tools mean European parts, and we ought to be buying American.

And goddamned sandals! You might as well be wearing a dress. Matter of fact in all of those sword and sandal epics that have been around forever, they are. If you had to be a man of action, chase down a mugger, defend your lady's honor, kick a carnivorous beast as he tried to rip you apart, would you want to do it in sandals?

Are we not men? What is the law?

I'm not that fucking angry.

৵৽৻৵

Time to check the mail. Sorry, not a winner.

৵৽৻৵

Why do I love baseball, and the Yanks in particular? Sure, it's the lore, the mystique, the rhythm of warm summer evenings, game in the background. It's all been said in much better language than I can muster but I love baseball because the seasons past have become the yardsticks of my life.

The sixty-nine Mets, we got to listen to it on the radio in the fourth grade, first few innings anyway. Fifty Catholic school kids and an iron-willed ogre of a woman, only non-nun in that grade at good old Blessed Sacrament. She was a Miss, though, so perhaps somewhat purer as a result.

My first game was with my dad, grandfather, and uncle, who almost caught me a ball. He dropped it and it was lost in the scrum.

I grew up in Brooklyn, learned to swim at the YMCA, played in the park; at night we'd have four or five different ice cream trucks. We'd wait for our favorite—Bungalow Bar. We'd play skelly by day and ring-a-levio until dark.

Being from Brooklyn, my entire family had been Dodger fans. They loved their Bums—'55, the year they'd won the series against the villainous Yankees, was a recent memory, a good one. Two years later they abandoned us. Us—I wasn't even born yet but I could feel the psychological vacuum all the same. Still do.

And to add to my hate list, I hate LA and the goddamned Dodgers. They should at least have given them a new name.

Then came the Mets. When I came in after dinner, the old man would often be found watching the game—or sleeping through it, Schmidt's in hand. The Mets went to the series, improbably, in '73. Buddy Harrelson, my dad's and my favorite Met, got into it with Pete Rose. Buddy got pummeled but he had balls. I met him years later at a charity golf event. He was a good guy. You guessed it—I liked him.

Tug McGraw bellowed, "You gotta believe!" Willie Mays played his last season as a player. We still had "Tom Terrific" and Jerry Koosman. We lost in seven games to a great Oakland A's team. I don't remember too many details but they put up a hell of a fight, took down the big red machine, and pushed the A's to the limit.

Then it was over. Mays retired. They didn't sign Harrelson and let Seaver and Koosman go. Tug McGraw want to the Phillies. The uniform was the same, but the team was ... Christ! We had a first baseman known as the Stork. Oh yeah, and Dave Kingman, a slugger who might hit forty home runs but he'd also hit a mere .220 and strike out 200 times a season. It sucked.

And then something happened. Chris Chambliss hit a walk-off home run, the Yanks won the pennant for the first time since '64, and the place went wild. I was hooked. They got swept by the Reds, came back the next year. Reggie Jackson hit three home runs to clinch the series in six games. Friggin' magic.

Then came '78.

12 | Another Letter

Seventeen days. A four-inch by four-inch metallic box with a swinging door. Open it up. Empty. I close my eyes. I see the empty box. What a metaphor—I hold the key to an empty box.

Snuck out to the golf course yesterday. Beer buddy asks if I've had word. "Nah," I say, "but I'm writing like hell."

He approves and says, "Maybe you should write her again. Maybe she didn't get it. Maybe the manager had a crush on her and threw your letter away."

"I could ask her the color of her eyes," I say half in jest.

"You don't know the color of her eyes?" he asks in disbelief. "After all this?"

"It was dark, and besides, there was a lot of other stuff to look at."

This wasn't entirely true but … . Yeah, it was. Who am I kidding?

Anyway, I think he was enjoying the story line and didn't want it to end. Neither did I. But write another letter? I swore to myself I wouldn't. I had one shot and I blew it. But maybe? Nah!

We played until nearly dark. On the way home I brought it up: "Another letter could be the killer. She might recoil, thinking me twice the jackass I'd already made of myself."

"She might not have gotten the first one," he nudged. "Or you might have to wait until next year."

He knew my soft spot. Another letter was an option. A quick road trip was another.

"Hey, I wrote you a letter. Did you get it? And by the way, what color are your eyes?"

And the road trip? "Hey, did you get my letter? Yes, I'm the jerk who wrote you. Yo, tell these big guys ... Hey, easy! No, you don't understand .."

I don't know. I sometimes wake at two or three in the morning and when my thoughts turn to her, she's grinding some other guy's knee. She got my letter, raised an eyebrow,

read half of it, and tossed it in a waste can.
What the hell am I after?

13 | '78

Spring of '78—I should have graduated high school. I didn't. Four years and I accumulated two credits, maybe two and a quarter. I don't remember, but it was bad. I'd been asked to stop coming in May. Nice meeting—myself and the principal. Handshakes, small talk. "There is no point in your continuing," he said.

I'd missed eighty-five days or so and when I did show up, I rarely attended class. Once in a while I'd show up and a startled teacher would eye me warily, as though I might contaminate the rest of the class. I didn't much care. I was always stoned in one form or another, sometimes fell asleep, and once or twice slid off a stool or desk. I was like a ghost who couldn't quite vacate the place.

Most of the time, I went in the front

door and out the back. School was where my friends could be found, where I copped my drugs, too. Not like I didn't try. Hell, I'd read my social studies and English books in the first week or two and then be bored shitless; math and science required work and I was too high for that.

So just like the year before, I got an early jump on summer. The year before I got shipped off to my grandparents' under the guise of a job in the city. The job didn't pan out, and I came home to find my dad had moved out. I got my years confused— '77 was the trippy summer, all summer, mister natural—three bucks a hit.

But in June of 1978 my grandfather came through with a real job. I'd have to live with them during the week, come home on weekends. I took the bait and hopped a train to Mineola.

Mineola was an ugly little suburban town thirty miles east of Manhattan. I was used to living in a rural potato growing town 100 miles east of Manhattan. My grandparents lived in an apartment. They set me up on a cot in the dining room. Gramps—yeah, that was what I called him—had been a general contractor, fairly successful. They'd left Brooklyn shortly after the Dodgers, bought a home in the suburbs, a bit farther out than their present location. He owned boats—his last was thirty-one feet— went on trips to Europe, the Caribbean. They had great parties.

Then he got sick. He was sick for a couple of years. I'll be honest, I'm not quite sure what it was, some type of infection that couldn't be knocked out. I don't know but this strong, no-nonsense Dutchman (he was German but his friends labeled him such) damn near died.

In the meantime his partner let the business go and retired to Florida. They had to sell the house, the boat. Family lore has it that he paid all of his creditors with the proceeds.

He recovered, and in his late fifties he got back in the game. He got a job as an estimator for a large Manhattan construction company. He wore a three-piece suit to work and was known as "Mister Cook." I was proud to be his grandson, though I never felt up to the part. Hey, I was a high-school dropout loser. We had been close once; as a kid he was a heroic figure to me. Tough, he'd boxed as a kid and had a cauliflower ear. He was the "Captain;" even his friends seemed to look up to him.

When I grew into my teens, grew my hair long, and wanted little more than to hang out and get high with my friends—well, it just wasn't the same.

My first day of work, Gramps and I walked to the train station together, boarded a train, changed at Jamaica. At Penn Station we walked to the Eighth Avenue subway line—maybe it was the Seventh—and I ended up at the Estee Lauder building across from the CBS studios. I think it was West 57th and 9th.

He introduced me to the crew I'd be working with—I was a laborer—and said, "See you tonight at home."

I was a month shy of my eighteenth birthday and on my own in the big city. My grandmother wanted to kill him. I did just fine. Next day I was on my own. He caught a later train.

A few weeks later word got out that I was Mr. Cook's grandson. My coworkers thought I might be a plant, a spy. I just didn't want to be treated differently. They bought it; it was true. They were an interesting crew.

There was Abe, a Jewish guy from Queens, with a Mitch Miller-type goatee. He was a good guy, helped me find my way home the first day. There was Jimmy, a little Italian guy of about sixty; brought fruit, cheese, and a little wine for lunch every day. He cut the fruit—apples, pears—with a large knife. Yeah, he ate bread, too. There was a big black guy and a skinny white kid from Bay Ridge who was working his way through college (don't remember him very well but he did introduce me to Kafka; the *Metamorphosis* was the book).

Three weeks later I was sent to a job to help a guy named Andy. Andy was a mason; he was black, from South Carolina.

We were pointing the brickwork (chipping out the old mortar and refilling the gaps between the bricks) on a building at West 63rd and Central Park West, across the street from the Mayflower Hotel before it was notorious. I think they tore it down.

Anyway, we were doing this pointing some fifteen to twenty stories above the ground. We'd hang some hooks off the parapets on the roof and lower a scaffold down with pulleys. No safety belts. The scaffold consisted of wooden planks. I was to mainly mix cement and lower tools in a bucket to Andy. Trouble was, I couldn't understand a word he said—thick accent. He had little use for me. First day, he sent me to Estee Lauder with a dolly and told me to bring back two 100-pound bags of cement. That was a hell of a trip, up and down curbs, across busy intersections, but when I returned, in pretty good time, I think, I earned a bit of respect. Within a week I was out on the scaffold with him. My grandmother was livid.

I worked with Andy the rest of the summer. We ate lunch on a bench by the park every day. I worked another job at One Fifth Avenue right on Washington Square; I was in reefer heaven. Andy and I became friends; he looked out for me. The city was a scarier place in 1978. I wore a hammer on my belt, had long hair, and people left me alone.

In July of 1978, the Yanks were 14½ games out of first place. They had a nut of an owner who fired managers, rehired managers, and fired them again; managers who nearly brawled with their own players; tons of ego and talent. By the All Star Break they were 7½ games back and climbing. In first place were the Red Sox, who had a helluva lot of talent in their own right. Yaz, Rice, Lynn, Fisk, Carbo, Remy—yeah, they were fun. I went to a Yanks-Sox game in July after the All Star Break. They played until 1:00 AM and then, because of an American League rule, since rescinded, they could not begin a new inning. The game concluded the next night. The Yanks lost, I think.

Living at my grandparents' wasn't great,

but they were good to me. We ate well, we watched baseball, and on Friday afternoons I took the train home, returning on Sunday evening long after they had gone to sleep.

My grandfather hated the Yankees. Most Dodger fans did. They had to; the Yanks had crushed them so often. He had embraced the Mets, somewhat halfheartedly, I sensed. That summer we watched a lot of Yankee games. He scowled but we watched. My grandmother seemed to enjoy it.

The New York newspapers went on strike that summer, in the middle of a goddamned pennant race. I bet a kid I knew $100 that the Yanks would win the pennant. A lot of money when I earned $2.50 an hour.

My grandmother left us alone for a week, going to California to visit a sister. We cooked, went out to dinner, to Roosevelt Raceway to see the trotters. One night we visited and had dinner with his elderly sister in Queens. She made calves liver with lentil beans, a German thing.

We bonded. I tried explaining the beauty of my favorite music. Christ, he didn't even like swing; it "had no melody." But he listened. He talked of life, family; he even touched on women a bit. This was not the man I thought I knew.

On the way home from his sister's a group of toughs in the street gave him some lip as we drove by. He stopped the car. I talked him out of it. "Let's go, Gramps, not worth it."

When the building superintendent, a guy named Jules who lived in a shitty apartment on the first floor, gave me some shit—he always stood by his door and eyed me up and down; he was a skinny little fuck with greasy hair and wore tank top tee shirts—that's right, he gave me some shit. I mentioned it to Gramps in passing. A few days later we were together and encountered Jules, and Gramps lit into him.

"Yes, Mr. Cook." He never bothered me again.

The summer passed, fall came, and my mom's sister suggested I could come live with them. You see, my mom lost our home to foreclosure and moved in with a friend.

My aunt would get me a job at Underwriters Laboratories. I'd be a blue collar—or more precisely, a brown collar—kid in a white collar world of engineers and such. The company would pay for any college classes I might take providing I got a C average. I would have to get an equivalency diploma. People had not yet given up on me.

My grandparents, though fond of me, encouraged me to try this path. My grandfather could have bought me a carpenter's apprentice book for five grand, but my aunt and uncle lived five miles from my old home. I missed my friends and off I went.

My aunt was my godmother. She and my uncle had always been good to me. She really stepped up here. I was lucky.

The Yanks came back, caught up in late September, went ahead, but the Sox came back, and on a sunny day—I think it was the first of October—they played a one-game, winner takes all. Bucky-fuckin-Dent. The great Yastrzemski fouled out, and the Yanks won the pennant. They stepped past the overmatched Kansas City Royals again, three years in a row, I think, and met the Dodgers in the World Series just like the year before.

I talked to my grandfather on the eve of the series. Son of a bitch if he didn't still love those Dodgers. How could he? But he did. We bet ten dollars on the series. The Yanks won. I never collected that bet.

Massive heart attack. We got the call, my aunt and I, on the morning of November 8, 1978. We rushed from work. I don't think she even told me what had happened— maybe she did—until we got there. He was gone. He was sixty-three.

People streamed through the funeral home, lining up to get in for two days. He was a hell of a guy.

I have his baseball glove, a 1920s style that he used when I was a kid and we played ball in the back yard. I thank God regularly for that summer and the chance to know the man. My grandmother became a die-hard Yankee fan, until the day she died at ninety-two. I miss them both.

14 | The Family Way, Part II

I put the pen down about 10:30, watched a bit of the ball game—they were on the West Coast and started at 10:00. I awoke at 2:00 A.M Saturday. No surprise what I was thinking of—thumpa, thumpa, bump, grind, titties, and beer. I didn't sleep a wink.

There is an unwritten code regarding these clubs. Maybe it is written. I've never seen it. You enter and leave reality behind. Beautiful and not-so-beautiful girls, wearing next to nothing, treat you like you're the most interesting guy they've ever met. You walk out the door and you're supposed to leave the fantasy behind, a great memory, and go back to being a schmo. For me it was like cruising along at 60 mph, the top down, tunes playing, feeling pretty good, and—damn, must have hit the ejector button, I'm sitting alongside the road with a sore ass watching my ride go on without me.

I wanted an order of that fantasy to go. I wish I could talk to my sister.

I have two sisters, though most people don't know that. Shit, for a good part of my life neither did I. My youngest sister lives not far away. We don't see too much of one another. I love her dearly and have all the shared memories of our somewhat rocky childhood. She's had her trials (who hasn't?) and come through them okay.

I remember the day she was born. I stood across the street from the hospital, Wykoff Heights, in Brownsville, I think. Bushwick? My mom held her up to the window. Shared holidays, photos, hurts, and memories.

My other sister—well, that was different. I'm twenty years old, working on a vegetable farm, cutting, picking, boxing. It was the only job I could find that summer. I'd returned from Florida a few months before, picked up the lousiest job I've ever had, a warehouse that sorted and moved automotive starters. When they fired me, I thanked them.

I was working in the field and up pops

my mother and her future husband, Bruno. She had something of great importance to lay on me: "You have another sister." I was sitting in the front seat of Bruno's Datsun pickup with my mom and Bruno. Bruno looked uncomfortable. My boss, Farmer Finn, is eyeballing me. I'm supposed to be working. What the hell do I say?

My mom was a piece of work. She had a flair for the dramatic and was the most manipulative person I've ever known. She also had many fine qualities. She gave me the gift of reading and did love me much. She did her best.

Apparently when I was real young, a year or less, my folks split up. She moved in with my grandparents, he with his sister. She dated, got pregnant, and did what all Catholic girls were expected to do back then—put the baby up for adoption. Sometime after that my folks got back together and proceeded to make each other miserable for the next fifteen years.

So my mom orchestrates a big get-to-know-ya. It was weird. I stood outside for an hour. My sister, Summer—not the name her adoptive parents had given her but one she chose for herself—was goddamned beautiful. She was eighteen, lithe of form, with long black hair. She was a topless dancer—that's what we called them back then— and she had a biker boyfriend. This guy epitomized the word dirtbag. He was about forty.

Well, it had been a rough week. My other sister took to her instantly. I was overwhelmed. My mom had a way of letting you know how you were supposed to feel, act, respond. I don't know who initiated contact but Mom was ecstatic. The harder my mom pushed, the more I recoiled.

I'd see Summer over the years. I'd sometimes put a little effort in, not too much, but I did try. I liked her. She was smart, funny, and pretty damned cool, but what might have sprouted into a relationship was pounded away by Mom's heavy hand. When I'd see Summer sporadically, it was always with a new boyfriend. They weren't a bad lot, easy enough to get along with. I'd see her at holidays. My awkwardness must have been damn near horrible for her, but she always maintained a grace and dignity. I was a dick. My mom looked at me, beseeching me—"It would make her so happy." I withdrew further.

When my mom got sick, pancreatic cancer, she had us all at the oncologist with her. She had center stage and we played our roles. The girls took care of her at home. I paid bills, behaved myself, but never gave her what she wanted. To this day I don't feel bad. I don't feel good either. We always had that relationship.

At her wake the minister—a woman with little talent for public speaking—read a eulogy my mom had written herself. It was, in brief, her life story. The fucking apple doesn't fall far from the tree, does it? When she got to the part about Summer— her conception, birth, etc.—I got up and stormed out. Mom had reached out from the grave. I had not in twenty years fully accepted the whole thing.

I didn't see Summer again until Grandma passed ten years later. She was still pretty damned cool. We talked. I said it was good to see her. I wanted to say more.

When I got back from Atlantic City. last year, I called her. In some strange way meeting Kerry made me feel closer to Summer. We got together in November, had dinner in a fancy place I'd plumbed a few years earlier. The owner had become a friend of mine; we got the first class treatment. I introduced her as my sister, for the first time. We parted friends, have spoken a few times since, and plan to get together again soon.

I wish I could talk to her about things, get her take on the situation, insights, advice. But I don't think I have that right. How fuckin' dare I?

∽⟨⟩∾

The hands on my back were strong; they kneaded, they pushed hard. "I'd forgotten how well you do this," I said.

"You haven't forgotten anything, honey," she responded.

I awoke to a splendid Sunday morning, Fathers' Day. I ain't nobody's daddy. Well,

I'm a doggy daddy. I get cards.

My back hurt. It was 8:30 A.M. I never sleep this late.

15 | Junk Mail

Four weeks since I saw her. Three weeks since letter sent.

I checked the mailbox yesterday, first time in a couple of days. I opened the door and there stood an envelope. The address was hand printed. I eyed it warily, heart racing a bit. I pulled it out.

```
Barbara Pringles
PO Box 151
South Port, NY 11971
```

Son of a bitch! Pull the goddamned rug out, why don't ya? I was pissed. A little while later I was bummed. Someone once told me that depression is rage turned inward. If the shoe fits ... it did. A wild night, a wild and crazy idea, four weeks of manic drive was subsiding. I could feel the pull of life, business, marriage weighing me back down to earth.

Whoever this woman was who previously got her mail in my box, I cursed her. I cursed the damned postal worker who put the letter in my box. I cursed myself for being an idiot. I cursed the girl who didn't write. Shit, I even cursed the guy who held the door for me as I stormed out of the post office.

16 | The Girl in the Hat, Part I

When I was twenty-one I met a girl, *the* girl. She was blonde, had eyes the color of turquoise. Maybe not, but in my mind's eye it's a pretty picture. She had a great figure. She had horses. Her father was a fisherman, his father a farmer. She was a country girl. She was fun. She liked to party. She was beautiful. She said things like, "Hells' bells." We were wonderful lovers.

She whispered in my ear in a moment of passion that she loved me, first time those words had ever been said to me. I'd never said them myself, not to a lover, girlfriend, friend. I loved her back and then some. I'd never felt so air-walking, moon-howling, heart-bursting happy as when I was with her. We didn't do much. We went to bars; we glowed; people were drawn to us. We went for walks in the snow. She took me riding. We Christmas-shopped at the flea market. Doesn't sound like much but those were among the best days I've ever known.

She gave me a cap and scarf for Christmas. The cap was of a type a cabby might wear, gray, it was. The scarf was emerald green. Thirty-three years later I still wear it and think of her, on winter nights walking in the snow. I wore it to both my mom's and grandmother's wakes over my tweed sport jacket. It means a lot to me.

It was brief and intense. I worked for a swimming pool company in the Hamptons. I drove a 1970 Volvo 144 station wagon. I lived at the "Hotel Crisp." This was an old farmhouse that had been inhabited by guys like me, twenty-something party animals, for years. There was actually a sign near the front door with the name, and a headless doll named (and labeled) Lucy, whose hands sometimes wandered. I lived there with Hank, a guy I'd known since my freshman year. He was a year or two older, had been in and out of the Marine Corps. He'd do two or three hits of blotter or mescaline to most civilians' one. He'd been in a bad accident a year or two earlier, half a mile from the house. His buddy—housemate— was killed. Hank had scars inside and out.

I met my love at the hotel. She came by to see Hank, had been his girl years earlier. He wasn't around. In fact, he'd become engaged to a girl we had both pursued. One night at a local pub I was on my way out to the parking lot with her to smoke a joint. He cut in with half a gram of blow. I was trumped. I think we had five bucks riding on the outcome. He won. He lost—she was a complete psycho.

Well, back to meeting Dawn— that was her name. We're hanging around, small talk. I break out a bottle of blackberry brandy. I think we killed it, had a great time. She left but there was a spark. I asked Hank about her and he gave me her number. I called; we went out Thanksgiving night. We clicked. By Christmas we were an item.

Things were good—great sex, great everything. Then I hit a rough patch. In the swimming pool business there's a dead season. Weather permitting we'd work right into December, get laid off to collect unemployment until March. I picked up some work off the books at the car wash. It sucked but it was work.

One morning on my way to work I hit a wall, a big brown wall. The driver of a UPS truck had pulled over to the shoulder of the eastbound lane of the two-lane road we were on. Whatever he was doing— checking paperwork, directions, picking his nose—he suddenly decided to make a hard left heading west. I lock 'em up, skid, and slam into his truck—T-bone—wrecked my car. I got no car, lose my job at the car wash, stuck at the hotel trying to negotiate a check from UPS. They did cut it in about a week. I was desperate and I guess they knew it. I got squat.

In the meantime, Hank's fiancée wants to move in, wants me out. I move into a local motel, seasonal weekly rental. I get a check, buy a piece of crap Mazda that blows up nine days later. Dawn comes by one day and says it's over. It was early February.

No job, no car, no girl. No one I knew

had a clue where I was, with the exception of some family. That motel room in the dead of winter was the worst place I've ever been. I was there about two more weeks. I wrote constantly, took the bus to town, wrote on the bus. I filled a notebook or two, then I stopped. For thirty-three years.

A couple of weeks later a friend came by, needed a housemate. My family came through, and I now had my second VW beetle. I went back to work in March. I wore my cap.

I called her once; she answered. I told her I missed her. "I miss you, too," she said. We've never spoken again.

One day that spring, I'm driving along on the expressway when alongside me is a black Z-28 Camaro. It's Bobby H., a guy I knew. He's a rich kid, had wrecked a handful of cars, thought he was Robert Plant. Shit, he'd even sung with my pals in the band a few years before (he bought the PA system). Well anyway, there he is alongside me, grinning from ear to ear, and guess who's sitting beside him. Yeah. I'm driving

a fucking beetle (actually, a Super Beetle).
I'm a captive audience. I salute and ease off
the gas. Dawn looked as though she wanted to disappear.

That's it. Not much of a romance, yet
I've never again known anything so sweet.
She had two younger brothers she was
very close to and a dog named Moonshine.
I had one picture of her, lost or possibly de-
stroyed by my wife years ago. In the picture
she was wearing a hat, a fedora-like thing.
I'd not thought of that photo until today,
not consciously. I also remembered how we
combined laughter with lovemaking.

We were wonderful lovers.

17 | A Plumber's Tale

I know it's been said in one form or another by a whole gaggle of humanity, but you can't know where you're going, or for that matter where the hell you are, if you don't remember where you've been. As I recall some of the people I've known, things I've done, and so on, they all lead to here and now. I'll try to be brief.

I've been a plumber for thirty years; I've been in business twenty-three years. I've owned a home for twenty-four years. I've been with the same woman for twenty-nine years and been married for twenty-five years. Aside from some weed, I haven't done drugs in twenty-seven years. The house we bought was a summer bungalow nestled in the woods with a fireplace and hand pump. We could see the creek from the driveway and walk to the bay in a matter of minutes.

It was the home I'd always imagined myself in. I've dreamed over the years, more than once, of having left this place behind, grieving the loss. I'm grounded here and walk the dogs to the creek daily. Over the years we fixed it up, put a second story on, added a deck, then a bigger deck, a pool, and the office.

I don't own a business—it owns me. I've been working seven days a week in one form or another for damn near thirty years. Shoot, I wouldn't own a home if I didn't. I've been working since I was twelve—paper route. I had my first employee at fourteen, a ten-year-old I hired to help me deliver each day. He ran my paper route when I got a job as a roofer's helper at fifteen. It was a summer job; I carried bundles of shingles up ladders, cleaned up, and even learned some roofing.

I drank beer at lunch and, on the way home, got paid once with Yates. I don't know what the hell they were but I hallucinated, ran into my worst enemy in the world, got the worst shit-kicking of my life but wouldn't go down. I could have taken the bastard any other day, but I couldn't make a fist I was so high.

I've worked every Saturday, it seems, for the last thirty-five years and enough Sundays to make it seem normal. My phone starts ringing at 7:00 A.M. and continues until 8:00 in the evening. I've got employees who sometimes work hard, sometimes don't, sometimes don't show up, are often late, and it's often like working with children.

My day starts at 7:00 A.M. and ends at 7:00 or 8:00 P.M. with my returning calls in the office. Too many people have my cell number because I am service mechanic, estimator, check collector, and whatever else needs doing. I still think I'm the best mechanic I've got. Sometimes I like owning a business. Sometimes I like helping people. Ever need a plumber?

I help people. The more they have, the cheaper they generally are, but some people, those with damn near nothing, I like to help. I do work for the local Methodist church. I don't charge them anymore. I'm not a member, but if I were to be a church-goer, the Methodists would have me. I grew up with all the bullshit and hypocrisy of the Catholics, the angry, red-faced nuns, and Christ, thank God I was a choir boy and not an altar boy.

When I was a Cub Scout and we met at the local Methodist church in Brooklyn, "Little Andrew," it was a happy and carefree environment. I went to a Sunday service there once, missing our Catholic service. They used to issue us envelopes to place our donations in and to keep track of our attendance. When I explained that I attend-ed the Methodist service instead, I caught holy hell. Yup!

I got married in a Methodist church. I was asked to be a trustee a few years ago at the church I do work for. I was honored, humbled. Not being a churchgoer or mem-ber, I did not feel worthy. I declined—a de-cision I kind of regret.

We had some good years through the housing boom of the late '90s and early

2000s. We've had some bad, real bad, years through the crash/recession. Things seem to be better now, and who knows what's to come?

So I got a nice home, a decent business. I work a lot, but so do most of the guys I know. The people I do work for, most are second-home owners and seem to have a lot of time off. Christ, they're always home, and my working at their homes speaks for itself. But I'm healthy and have plenty of work. I am blessed.

I've many friends, some through golf, some through work—guys I work with or for as a subcontractor, some customers, people I've known for years, watching their children grow and their dogs and homes and, for that matter, their selves growing old like me. People who've imparted their wisdom, sorrows, perspectives, the fabric of lives I'm privileged to know.

I have a special friend, two I suppose— my dogs. Polly is a dog. In every sense she's a dog—not too bright, she clamors for attention and waves her tail at the slightest sign of notice. She is a matronly, benign presence. I think of her as Mrs. Butterworth ... never mind.

Zeke is another story, 120 pounds of long-haired German shepherd. He is magnificent. Beautiful, smart, and strong. He has a sense of humor. We are bonded. He had back surgery as a pup, an infection on the spine. I had to carry him, his hind legs in a sling. He was too much dog for my wife and had to go to work with me frequently. We were quite the pair. He's eight now, travels with me less frequently. I've had and loved many dogs over the years, but he's special. They have such a short time with us, and it will be a dark time when he goes. I treasure every walk, every day.

I've beaten around the bush long enough, I guess. I've been with my wife a long time. I'd dated, hung out with, had relationships with a lot of women—some rather wonderful in their own right— after Dawn. No one quite measured up. I met my wife at twenty-five. She was thirty-five but in many ways younger and more childlike than I. We started together in a coke-y haze but we grew, I first, I think. I just stopped, no program, no meetings. I just stopped, got my shit together as the saying goes. She followed.

We fit together, we grew together, we stuck together. We married, formed a life. We had good and bad times but the good outweighed the bad. The years went by. There were always times of darkness in her moods, but we were able to pull through. I've spent thirty-plus years at her side. We've laughed, loved, hurt together. I've always been able to make her smile, laugh. Lately, I fear my act has grown old.

Do I think I was the great love of her life? No. She had married at seventeen, high-school sweetheart, divorced a few years later with two kids. She was a lovely waif of a girl from the photos I've seen. No, I think there was a guy with long hair and a mustache she loved some ten years before me. She told me sparingly of him over the years. Funny, he drove a Triumph TR-6.

We built the business, built or rebuilt

our home, built our life. She hit rough patches and with great tenacity recovered, although it seemed she lost a little of herself each time. She had a rough time in '07 and has lost ground steadily since. I can't make her smile, let alone laugh, any more. I've spent a lifetime or so it seems holding her up, picking her up, shielding her from hurt as best I can. When asked how she fared, I would often present a picture of normality. I would try to protect both of us from the stigma, the perceptions of the outside world. We loved one another deeply, still do, though we both seem to be terribly unhappy.

Recently her daughter, a woman with a fair share of troubles in her own right, has moved into our home. I had reservations, still do, but she has helped out a great deal with her mom. She helps keep house; we eat less takeout and they keep each other company. I have felt my emotional burden lift a bit. My wife still doesn't get out much; consequently, neither do I. Back below ground, the safety of the hole greets me.

That sucked. I had to get through that, but if it sucked to read it, it was worse to write. I have cared for, loved, and nurtured this woman for a long time. Abandonment is not in the picture. I'll always be there for her. She's been sinking for years and pulling me under as she goes.

18 | What's Next?

This whole thing with Kerry/Charger was maybe me reaching out as I went under, grabbing for the banks, a branch, a hand. Help me! Right. She was never going to write me back. It was folly from the get-go, but for damn near a month I've looked up—unrealistically, foolishly, insanely—but up it was. What now?

What's next for the damned old fool? Answer the question. Has he been chasing the same girl for thirty-some odd years? Would I be willing to suffer another thirty years for a night, a week, a lousy month or two if by some quirk of fate Kerry had responded? Bet your ass I would! Ain't happening. A month of empty mailbox viewing has attested to that.

Would a second letter be in the works? Wasn't the first bad enough? A field trip? Maybe. Who knows? Time will tell. A month of immersion in the day-to-day of my life has cooled the passions that gave life to this story to begin with.

Would I return to Atlantic City. a month, six months from now, ask her if she got my letter, settle the mystery of her eye color? I don't know. May be the makings of another story. One thing for sure, if I live another year, if Gerry Cooney doesn't kill me first, and I return on a golf trip next spring, this old Hemingway-looking son of a bitch, like a moth to a flame, will go back looking for a hat, a girl, a memory. I'd tell her again what wonderful lovers we'd be.

Did I really expect her to write back? Yes. Did I want a friend? A date? A relationship? A day in the park walking hand in hand? Someone to talk to? Yes, yes, yes, yes, and yes!

I liked the way I felt when I was with her. I like the way I feel when I think of her. I still lose sleep, particularly Fridays and Saturdays. I lie in bed and she's—well ....

I didn't want to let her go that last night in the club. I don't want to let her go now.

Each day I lose a little piece. Writing of her has kept it alive, real.

Is she really sweet? Nice? Is her name really Kerry? Maybe it's all lies. Christ, she could be Donna from fucking Camden. Does it really matter? I'll have to get back to you on that.

Meanwhile, I'll check the box—what the hell?—bury myself in work, count my blessings, and carry on. Life may still have some surprises in store for me. I hope they are good ones.

Like the girl in the hat.

Made in the USA
Middletown, DE
20 April 2021